# 108
# TEACHINGS

# 108
# TEACHINGS

Esoteric Himalayan Wisdom and
The Path to the True Self

## Yogmata Keiko Aikawa

HIMALAYAN WISDOM SERIES

Natus Books
Barrytown, NY

Published by Natus Books
120 Station Hill Road
Barrytown, NY 12507

Natus Books is a publishing project of the Institute for Publishing Arts, Inc., 120 Station Hill Road, Barrytown, NY 12507, a not-for-profit, tax-exempt organization [501(c)(3)].

Cover and interior design by Susan Quasha

ISBN: 978-1-58177-180-0

Library of Congress Control Number: 2019942155

Manufactured in the United States of America

# CONTENTS

# INTRODUCTION
## A Message from Yogmata

## True Spirituality: Returning to the Essential Self through Meditation

The word *spirituality* has become part of our popular culture, yet its essential meaning often eludes us. We are all spiritual beings, born with a body and mind, and yet we are intrinsically nonphysical. We come from and belong to a sacred source that is both infinite and timeless. True spirituality leads back to this sacred source and ultimately reconnects us to our True Selves. It is here, beyond the intellect and within the innermost part of our selves, that we become one with the divine. I call this divine force God, the origin of all creation. Others might consider it a super-consciousness or an omnipotent and omnipresent source of the universe.

Whatever we choose to call it, we are all microcosms composed of the same essence as the universe. We are not merely the body and the mind. This misconception is at the root of enduring pain and suffering. On an external level, we are stuck in our egos, constantly seeking fulfillment through the senses and relinquishing our connection to this sacred source. The ego is attached to deep-seated fears and material desires that attract mental clutter like a magnet, obscuring the truth. It is reactive and changes every moment in its pursuit of self-satisfaction.

Operating at the level of ego and seeking personal glory in the material world generates tremendous stress, anxiety, and conflict. We make judgments based on narrow personal experiences. We simultaneously defend, doubt, and distrust ourselves and others. Eventually, this state-of-being is like living in a house of cards: we continue on this false path with its short-term gratifications until, often with sudden swiftness, things fall apart.

True healing and inner peace can only occur when we clear out the mental clutter and emotional roadblocks that we have accumulated through past experiences and incarnations. We must become aware of the ego, purify it, and return to the sacred source, where we have access to infinite consciousness.

## The Transformative Power of Esoteric Himalayan Wisdom

Esoteric Himalayan wisdom is the path to this transcendent healing and true spirituality; it is established through harsh ascetic training that explores the mind, body, and soul through Samadhi. Also referred to as "satori" or "enlightenment," samadi is defined by Hindu teachings as the realization of the ultimate state of consciousness. It involves literally transcending body, mind, and spirit through deep meditation. In this state, one becomes a pure being beyond karma and has access to profound unseen realms of knowledge. Those who have achieved this state of Samadhi are known as Siddha masters.

Since ancient times, Siddha masters have retreated to underground caves for this ascetic practice and entered the Samadhi state for days without any contact with the outside world. True Siddha masters have preternatural control over their physical senses and can enter Samadhi at any time. In so doing, they are bestowed with metaphysical wisdom about the universe, consciousness, and God. Ultimately, through the pure and transcendent energy of Samadhi, Siddha masters discover the sacred truth and are able to serve as a bridge between human beings and God.

Samadhi is the highest state of evolution of human consciousness and the most difficult of the many ascetic yoga trainings that have existed for millennia. In lesser-known regions of the Himalayas, Siddha masters never leave the mountains or mix with society. Pilot Baba is the most famous Siddha master in India, regarded by countless followers as a "Living Buddha." After many years as a yoga master and author committed to teaching and healing others, I had the good fortune to be invited by Pilot Baba to undergo rigorous training in the Himalayas. In 1986 I became the first and only woman to experience Samadhi, attain enlightenment, and become a Siddha master. From that point on, I have been committed to spreading the truth to hundreds of thousands of people all over the world.

## Meditation: The Path to Healing, Happiness, and Universal Love

Encountering a Siddha master who has reached Samadhi is rare. When you connect to a Siddha master like me by attending a darshan or receiving a diksha, you are spiritually awakened and purified.

*Darshan* is a Sanskrit word which means auspicious viewing. It is an opportunity to meet and share the same space with a master or spiritual guide. Through their gaze—through their presence beside you, the physical touch of their hands, as well as direct and indirect shaktipat—a blessing occurs that facilitates your safe and swift transformation in this lifetime. After darshan, people often experience inner warmth and radiant happiness. Anger dissipates. Sometimes people are moved to tears even though they are not sad. At other moments they may experience a tingling sensation in their bodies.

If you are not prepared for spiritual transformation, you may not feel much initially at darshan. However, an imperceptible shift is still happening at a deep level. The more you attend darshan, the more blessings you receive and the more steadily you experience happiness.

A diksha is a spiritual initiation that connects one to supreme conscious energy. During this ceremony, a Siddha master cleanses one's karma, transmits energy from the source of the universe, and bestows a mantra as part of the teaching of esoteric meditation. This meditation has a profound effect on the mind and body. The body is a microcosm comprised of different vibrational energies; Himalayan esoteric teachings and meditation purify, evolve, and ultimately transcend these different forms of energy and open the door to the True Self. Meditation awakens one's divine nature and facilitates one's journey on the road to becoming a free, conscious person. Relaxing the mind, it also rapidly purifies the senses and fosters within an absolute stillness that is as deep and expansive as the ocean.

Sage daily use of the body and mind actually prepares us for meditation. We can also prepare ourselves for meditation by acting morally in our daily lives, by not hurting anyone with our words, thoughts, or actions, and by expressing love, gratitude, and respect to everyone, including ourselves. This enhances the flow of positive energy on every level. Since meditation deals with internal energy, it is dangerous to experiment with different methods when we meditate. Siddha masters have a thorough knowledge of energy and secret keys to awakening the body and mind. Their guidance is the most rightful path in life.

Even if you visit the innermost sanctum of the Himalayas, it is likely to be mere mountain climbing. Siddha masters like myself offer opportunities to help you transform as quickly as possible, not by traveling to the Himalayas, but as you go about your daily life. Anyone can transform more intensively and scientifically—and more easily—this way than they can by going to the Himalayas. Sharing the love of Siddha masters like myself helps people overcome karma, forge their own destinies, and transcend the ego.

Through hundreds of thousands of reincarnations, human beings accumulate memories of karmic experiences. These experiences form and determine our individual character and personal role in life. Though we are destined to suffer through karma, an encounter with our True Selves can set us free from a life of disillusionment. Himalayan wisdom reveals who we are on an intrinsic level, which frees us to live more creatively and with abundant joy. As our inner peace becomes more expansive, we get closer to the source of our True Self. This is our journey back to the source of our birth. It is our journey home.

## 108 Teachings: Sacred Words and Life Principles

This book consists of 108 teachings or principles. The number 108 is sacred in many religions and traditions. In Japanese Buddhist temples, a bell is chimed 108 times to finish the old year and herald the new one. One hundred and eight is the number of major energy channels in the microcosm that, when cleansed, help us purify earthly desires. This is familiar to many Japanese people. One hundred and eight is also the number of prayer beads on a mala.

I pray that these 108 teachings heal your pain and sorrow, encourage you, and bring you closer to the truth. You are free to start with any one of them, but my hope is that you read from the beginning, since each teaching is meaningful. As you proceed, you will likely be drawn to a few, particular teachings. Read what sentences that impress you over and over again.

You can also intuitively turn to a page and read one message each day. Each message has its own meaning. Do not construe the one you happen to pick that day as a prediction; simply ponder and cherish each one. Some passages may move you; others may not. The message that moves you is perhaps what you need most at the moment. When you come across passages that don't interest you, accept the fact that you don't understand them and don't use your mind to try to do so. The more you move along in the book, the more mental clutter will be lifted away.

This book is infused with words of truth that emerged through Samadhi. They might shake you up and touch your soul, or you may feel nothing because your mind is filled with distractions. Even so, you will still receive something at the level of your soul that will eventually transform your consciousness and generate inner peace without dissipating your energy. You will eventually understand why you were born and why you are alive and find the true enlightened path that leads to happiness. This book is imbued with that level of transformative power because its content was created not through the mental machinations of my mind, but in the transcendent state of Samadhi.

One of the essential messages in this book is simple yet profound: love your True Self, get in touch with the sacred source, find your center, and live with unwavering faith. It is imperative that we all understand and experience this wisdom in order to create a better world—one that is grounded in love and peace. If you read this book over and over and ponder it with your eyes closed, love will gradually radiate within. Your connection to your spiritual self will deepen and your mind will become purified and healed.

Being unconditionally compassionate to others without expecting anything in return is another essential step that works in tandem with meditation. This encourages others to commit to the same path and generates more peace in the world at large.

I sincerely hope that this book inspires you to raise your awareness, get healed, and, above all, practice meditation. This will open the door to a greater sense of purpose in life, more meaning, and joy. It is my greatest hope that we all find our inner light, raise our consciousness, and experience universal love, wisdom, peace, and compassion. I am here to awaken you and guide you to this light. Let us take a first step in that direction.

YOGMATA KEIKO AIKAWA
August 2012

# 108
## TEACHINGS

# 1

## Release unnecessary thoughts

We all seek happiness in life. However, sometimes we get caught in the seduction of expressing the difficulties and hardships we experience in life. This might bring momentary relief, but without raising our consciousness, we are bound to repeat the same patterns and, thus, encounter the same difficulties and hardships.

Relying solely on the mind creates unproductive mental clutter. It is futile to worry or hope for positive outcomes. When we are stuck in the mind, we chart the same course on the same sea, perpetually sailing in the same place over and over again.

Release unnecessary thoughts. True growth comes when we purify the mind and become conscious of the mind's power to sway us. This awareness liberates and releases us from the tyrannies of the mind. It also cultivates an awareness of the limitations of temporal reality. When we release the mind's clutter, we move beyond the constraints of time. The present moment becomes part of an unchanging eternal present Now. When we have achieved this state of consciousness, we transcend both time and space, and return to the True Self.

## 2

## The mind is cunning

People often seek approval and often get defensive out of fear. The mind is cunning and deflects criticism as a means of self-defense.

Everyone enjoys praise, but often praise only serves the ego. When we connect to the truth, we are empowered enough to transcend the need to satisfy the ego. We become freer, more caring people. An awareness of the cunning nature of the mind creates harmony and well-being, which has a positive impact not only on ourselves, but on those around us.

Nature is abundant and unconditionally generous. Flowers are beautiful not because they seek acknowledgment; they bloom and are fulfilled from within. When we connect to the sacred source of life, we are gratified in the same manner. We, too, bloom and are fulfilled from within.

## 3

## Only love exists at the deepest level

Many of us are preoccupied by what we lack. We all want love and praise. We want material comforts. This is ego-driven love, motivated by desire.

However, beyond this ego-driven love there is great, infinite love all around us. It is universal love and natural energy that informs everything, including water and air. Everything is powered by love. This universal love also exists within us, since we are microcosms of the universe.

There is only love. We live with, by, and for love. We must be grateful for this eternal love. With gratitude, we become aware of this omnipresent love and experience inner peace, fulfillment, and grace on a profound level.

# 4

## Trust others

Serious people have a strong sense of responsibility and often try hard to be independent. When we are serious-minded but feel unmotivated or despondent, we need to ponder the infinite blue sky and create space in our minds.

To succeed, we do not have to do everything by ourselves. You don't have to bear your burdens alone. Place trust in others and share with love. Let us release the burden of doing everything on our own and leave things to the sacred source that is deep within us all. The people around you will help you, which will in turn evolve themselves.

Having a life is as important as making a living. Life is more vibrant and fulfilling when we connect to the sacred source. When we become one with the sacred source, we experience the truth, the sovereignty of love and wisdom, and from within we emit a mysterious power and cultivate the ability to endure.

# 5

## Daily mindset is important

What emotions do you feel every day? We often perceive others well but don't perceive ourselves in the same fashion, despite what we think. If we always lament and bemoan the imperfections of others, we will not be aware of our own imperfections.

When you meet others, what kind of feeling do you have? Our feelings toward others often cycle back to us. Our daily mindset is paramount in offsetting this condition. We must cultivate respect and empathy for others. This empowers us to attract and transmit positive energy. If you give good things to others with courage and love, you will become lighter, clearer, and more at ease.

## Embrace differences

Anger is universal. We often get irritated or annoyed when other people's ways of thinking conflict with our own. This accumulates and eventually becomes anger. Sometimes this anger can be directed against ourselves. To avoid conflicts and antagonism, it is best to release anger and literally blow it away. When you can't release anger in the moment, in private you can let out a big voiceless sigh with your mouth wide open.

How else can we manage anger? One solution is to understand its source. What is right for us is often not right for others. How we are raised, how we feel in the moment, and the priority we assign things are part of the equation. People have different values. People are diverse. If we are aware of this and observe the flow of our anger energy, that energy will be spontaneously released and dissipate. Further progress is achieved when we transcend the mind, become one with love, and release attachments.

# 7

## Laugh

We all experience a diverse range of emotions. In fact, we often think that life without emotions is boring. Of all the emotions, laughter has the power to release dark energy. Try laughing right now for ten seconds. Your mind and your emotions will lighten up.

Deeply distressed people, however, cannot laugh easily. Even during weeklong meditation retreats with daily meditation practice, they're not able to laugh with ease. But when they are purified and transformed through deep meditation, their mental load is lightened, and they eventually surrender to natural, joyful laughter. Good fortune comes to those with a sense of humor. Laugh and the world laughs with us. Being too serious prevents levity.

When we purify the mind through deep meditation to encounter the True Self, we experience the infinite essence that exists on a deep inner level. This essence has no fear, is all-knowing, and exists in a realm beyond our emotions (joy, anger, pathos, and humor). When we reach this state of consciousness, we become joyful people without suffering. However, our True Selves transcend even this state of consciousness.

# 8

## Forgive yourself

Frailty may seem refined and mournfully beautiful, like the sad splendor of a tragic heroine in a film or at the theatre. However, when we are overwhelmed with sadness and negativity, we can get chronic and serious illnesses. Our life force is depleted, and our negativity can even deplete other people's energy.

To re-empower us with life force, we must not blame ourselves. Instead, we must practice forgiveness. Love yourself and express gratitude toward everything around you. Look within. Perhaps you harbor the false notion that sadness is what you deserve. Forgive yourself. It's okay to be happy.

Do not hesitate to experience joy. Laugh and be happy. Reclaim your life power. No matter what we do or what we achieve, there will always be sadness unless we connect to the True Self. Only then can we experience immense happiness and life force with the restorative power to heal and cure everything.

# 9

## The extreme pleasure

Pleasure is an important concept with many phases, from ordinary pleasure to deep, profoundly meaningful pleasure. The deepest stage of pleasure is the nirvana that comes with enlightenment, when the mind is completely purified and free from attachments. This is the extreme pleasure of freedom—the state of mind that comes when we have transcended the senses, including the mind and body. Real happiness comes when we cultivate peace of mind without craving.

What kind of pleasure do you indulge in? You might enjoy the pleasure of alcohol or tobacco, or other substances. You might enjoy doing whatever you want in the moment, according to your whims. No matter what your inclination is, beware: sensual pleasures without consciousness are all-consuming and never-ending. When we enjoy sensual pleasures without being fully conscious, we cultivate unyielding attachments. Our mind and body get off-balance, which in turn creates suffering. Tobacco and alcohol are a major example of this. Through meditation, we become aware of these attachments and can release them. Connecting to your True Self brings inner peace.

## 10

### Egoless happiness

When our wishes are fulfilled, we experience joy. We impart that happiness to others and share our expansive compassion. The happiness that comes through shared joy also purifies the mind and fills the world with peace and love. This is not happiness of the ego or of self-gratification.

Accepting the joy of others without our egos brings happiness to the whole of society. Let us also understand that everything that happens around us is not about winning or losing, but a learning opportunity imbued with the grace of a power greater than ourselves.

We tend to suffer because we look at life through the polarity of winning and losing. This, in turn, creates envy, sadness, or depression. Through ego-less love we can act with more refinement and sophistication. Seeking ways to please the ego can be exhausting. Transcend this mindset and imbue yourself with true love and deep silence.

# 11

## Recognize and free your anger

When things don't go our way, we get irritated in different ways. Sometimes our irritation is suppressed; other times, it's explosive. When people do things differently from us—when we experience misconceptions, dashed expectations, or failure—we get aggravated, with ourselves or with others. When this persists, anger becomes habitual. It strains our hearts or creates anxiety. Irritation can be exhausting and self-perpetuating. The more irritation we experience, the greater that irritation becomes. Eventually, our minds and bodies, as well as our overall energy, grow weary. This can create illness.

Anger does not solicit apologies or forgiveness. Instead, it creates misunderstandings and negativity. Anger is unproductive, but it can change when we are conscious and understand it. When we release the attachment of our egos, we release the vice grip of anger.

Take a deep breath, relax, and release desire. Nothing changes without consciousness. Observe your breath and try not to be influenced by your anger or the anger of others.

# 12

## Observe the source of your sadness

When someone important to us passes away, sadness overwhelms us and endless tears flow. We must explore whether we are crying for them or if our ego is experiencing the sadness. When we're overcome with grief or sadness, we become weak. Our vital energy dissipates. To some extent, having a good cry frees us from deep sadness, but we must try to move forward. Life isn't only filled with sadness, but sadness is a process from which we can learn and develop.

We are loved by an invisible being. Let us observe what exists behind the feeling of sadness. Living at the mercy of emotion is painful. Understand your emotions, transform them into joy, and try to transcend them. Sadness, anger, joy, and pleasure are all learning experiences. When we are able to transcend these experiences, we are free. With trust and the blessing from Samadhi, we encounter the True Self.

This experience transforms consciousness and opens the door to a life of love and peace.

## Anger is our own problem

People get angry when they're hurt by others. Being hurt is experienced by the ego, and since this anger is tenacious and often feeds on itself, it is difficult to forgive others. Some people silently bear grudges and resentment for a long time. One reason we get angry is because we unconsciously have within us that which we cannot accept in others, which incites our anger in the first place. We react because someone else reveals what we dislike about ourselves. In other words, it is our own problem. When you can't forgive others and lose your temper, at least forgive yourself and love the part of you that is angry. Treat others not with anger.

When we get angry, we experience and are damaged by the toxic energy of anger. In those moments, we must accept ourselves and also thank the person who provoked our anger in the first place. This is an opportunity to release the negative stronghold of our ego and the attachments of our mind. Awareness and gratitude are transformative and transmitted to others on a deep level as love. This, in turn, facilitates change in others.

# 14

## Your gentleness is helping others

Some people easily inflame other people's anger. They are easily subjected to the wrath and temper tantrums of others. Perhaps we are kind and do not like to fight. For this reason, others can speak frankly to you. In fact, anger is a catalyst for change. You help others by giving them the space to express and release their feelings of anger and discontent. When you find yourself becoming the target of other people's anger, remember that you are, in fact, helping others by letting them vent, express their negative energy, and get in touch with their emotions. God, the invisible presence, is watching both parties equally. Instead of blaming yourself or hating the person who expressed themselves so candidly, consider in a positive light the fact that they expressed a frank, direct opinion. Thank them and convert this into an opportunity to cultivate more awareness. Take it as a learning experience and move on. In so doing, you will reinforce your ability to handle similar situations.

This can also be a catalyst for understanding that different people perceive things in different ways. It is also an opportunity to become aware of feelings in your own sub-consciousness that you didn't know existed. Other people are mirrors for us. They reflect ourselves back at us. Do good deeds so that positive energy is mirrored back to you. Be grateful for everything, clear your mind, and meditate on transformation. This will empower you.

# 15

## See things simply as they are

What sort of daily thoughts do you have? Are you angry, sad, upset, depressed, or anxious? Do you feel superior, compare yourself to others, or obsess over specific things that somebody mentioned that you can't get out of your head? Do you mull over these things over and over again? The mind reacts whenever something happens. These reactions of the mind are generated by the ego. The mind reacts when the ego is hurt.

People believe that they are their egos and therefore engage in egocentric thinking. But your ego is not your True Self. When you mistake your ego for your True Self, you are never able to step outside your ego. You end up tyrannized by your ego, which generates suffering and self-blame.

When you notice that your mind is reactive, recognize that this is provoked by your ego and observe it from a distance. Just observe it as a fact.

# 16

## Love turns the other cheek

We all want to love and be loved. It seems impossible, however, to be loved by everyone in this world. Our competitive society is based on winning and losing. Many of us protect our own interests above all else, which makes us aggressive whenever our position or place in the world is threatened.

Jesus Christ said, "If someone strikes you on the right cheek, turn to him the other also." This means that instead of attacking back we should forgive others and send love in return. This might be difficult for you, but when others release their emotions by attacking you, they will eventually feel remorse for their behavior.

When you transmit love back to someone who has attacked you, they are obliged to observe themselves. They become conscious of their actions and experience more empathy. May you always radiate the welcoming energy of love and gratitude in all situations.

# 17

## Radiate love and respect without comparing

We can't help but compare. The world is a competitive place. We all unknowingly perceive and compare superficial things: our economic status, physical appearance, level of education, social status, and so on. We often vacillate between feeling superior and feeling depressed.

The mind is always working and comparing. By understanding, purifying, and transcending the mind, we can live at peace with an expansive view of life. The mind does not impede us from interacting with others with compassion.

First, observe how you compare yourself to others. Accept the part of yourself that compares, as well as others who do the same. Then try not to compare. Instead, radiate love and respect. That's how we make our lives shine and express its radiance to others. Furthermore, pray for another person's happiness. This is the path to enlightenment.

We are at the mercy of our minds, which are unconscious and insatiable. By understanding who we are and not being swayed by our minds, we approach enlightenment. This is the true way to live and make our lives shine.

# 18

## Everything comes down to gratitude

No matter how hard your life is, accept everything as a learning experience rather than complain. It is important to express gratitude for this God-given knowledge. When you comprehend the inner energy that infuses all human beings, you become more aware of this knowledge. Educated people have a tendency to compare and analyze at the level of the mind. Let us break this entrenched habit and strive instead for a universal, non-judgmental view of life. We will be rewarded with the opportunity to experience love, peace, and well-being.

We will also understand the laws of nature and life. Are we living with love, forgiveness, gratitude, affirmation, and a creative, open mind? Let us release attachments to what is good and bad. Instead, let us live in the moment naturally and peacefully with an empty mind. Let us experience this state of consciousness whether we are loving ourselves the way we are, forgiving others, or expressing gratitude to those around us.

# 19

## Love yourself and forgive all

Feeling negative is actually an opportunity to clear your mind, because what you've suppressed is ultimately coming to the surface to be explored and released. In these moments, forgive and love yourself.

Nobody wants to lose in life. Sometimes we blame others. Other times we blame ourselves. When we see something white, the mind tells us that it is too white. When we see something red, the mind tells us that it is too red. The mind always changes and rarely accepts the middle path. It always sways between plus and minus energy; between negative and positive polarities.

When you clear your mind and connect to your True Self, feelings of gratitude emerge from a deep inner place. It is like the gratitude we experience when the rain provides vital water to plants, or when the sky is a radiant, beautiful blue. It is even akin to the simple gratitude we experience when buses and trains arrive and depart with regularity.

Love yourself and forgive everything. The positive and negative polarities that tyrannize your mind will balance out and lead you to the third energy of silence.

# 20

## How to eliminate all problems

When a family member becomes ill or other problems arise, we often experience worry, anxiety, or confusion. This, however, only creates a toxic situation. We must learn to accept family problems as a lesson for our personal evolution. It's hard to change others, but once you change yourself, your family will begin to change as well. The illness of a family member can improve eventually, and problems can resolve themselves even without your direct intervention.

Purify yourself with humility and trust, and commit yourself to God, the eternal essence of the Source. A strong bridge is required between you and this source in order to achieve this state of grace. A Samadhi master—a reliable spirit who has become one with God and the source—can be that bridge. When you directly or indirectly ask this spiritual guide to pray, your prayers are transmitted to the sacred source at the level of God, through *sankalpah*, which is an expression of ultimate intention. Prayers are answered in this way and miracles happen. You need to trust and love profoundly and leave things to fate.

# 21

## Be aware of yourself

The path to the truth is a journey toward the essence of the source of wisdom, peace, and power. This journey starts through purification and awareness. Karma is the accumulation of memories of actions from passed lives. We all have different ways of seeing, feeling, and understanding—whether in a positive or negative light, with or without judgments—according to our own karma.

We have no time to lose in our quest to reach the sacred source, where we experience our True Self. There are many alluring, delicious, and beautiful distractions in this world, both in our personal and professional lives. Many of us are preoccupied with and deeply attached to these things. Although they might nurture the mind and body, they distract us from the path toward our True Self. By preventing us from understanding our true purpose in life, these distractions consume much of our energy and often generate worry and anxiety. Cultivate awareness of these pre occupations and attachments in the mind. Try to understand how you perceive and understand the world around you. Observe exactly what you see right now. Are you fully aware of what your eyes perceive? Are you fixated on a sound or a smell? Try to discern how you feel when you see. Do you perceive the activity of the mind?

# 22

## Observe your inside at every moment

We are all on a journey of natural evolution. We all seek a better life while we struggle with the basics, such as keeping cold and hunger at bay.

Encountering the truth through the wisdom of Samadhi opens the door to a different way of living and helps us evolve into more enlightened beings. It is a deeply fulfilling way of life that instills in us the capacity to experience life on a profoundly spiritual level. It nurtures the truth, virtue, and beauty within.

Many of us still don't know who we are. Our sense of True Self is obscured by anger, desire, ignorance, suspicion, doubt, hatred, and the agony that comes from not knowing love. These are the inflated preoccupations of the ego. Observe what you are feeling at every moment. You suffer because you are fixated on your own thoughts.

Our salvation from such a problematic way of life lies in the swift evolution of our consciousness. Through the wisdom of Samadhi, a life of taking from others as a form of self-defense becomes a life of giving as an expression of love. Sacredness is gradually awakened, and we're able to share and experience unconditional love. This is not an expression of the ego. Rather, it is the only natural way of living.

## Trust allows energy to flow

When people trust each other, good energy is exchanged. Once one of them has doubt, that flow of good energy is obstructed. There is an infinite God in all of us. This is the condition of our True Self and our pure essence. An encounter between two people is not just an encounter; it is a learning opportunity bestowed by God.

Trust and face others. Trust allows positive energy to flow again. Peace without doubt or fear creates a warm and hospitable atmosphere. If this is hard to achieve, it is because we don't trust ourselves. We must first trust the relationship we have with ourselves. When we dislike ourselves, energy does not flow smoothly. When we express negative energy in the form of doubts, we receive negative energy in return. On the other hand, when we trust ourselves, we are, in turn, trusted by others. On one level we create everything that we receive. In India, people first join their hands in prayer when they meet others. They pray for the God that they know resides in others. When they encounter others with trust, they open the door to the flow of positive energy.

# 24

## Get selfless love from the master

We all unknowingly accumulate stress and use our physical senses too much. We tend to be full of demands. When we get sensory overload, we also get emotionally paralyzed, lose balance, become ill or anxious. When we connect to a spiritual guide who is a bridge to the love of the Source, however, we are centered and feel at ease. If we build unshakable trust in this journey of evolution, we will always be fulfilled, even when we are separated from our spiritual guide.

There needs to be a strong connection of love between you and your spiritual guide or master, who loves everyone equally, just as the sun shines light for all. When we are stuck inside our minds, we only see what we believe and can never see what radiates around us. When the mind becomes empty, we experience love from the sacred source and understand the nature of life.

# 25

## A joyful life

What makes life joyful? Cooking is exciting: playing with flavors and tastes, trying out different ethnic cuisines, improvising with whatever you have in your kitchen. Similarly, thinking creatively is joyful and fun. Let us engage in life as creatively as possible every day. Instead of dwelling on negative energy, take action and express yourself creatively.

Intense joy comes when we are our True Selves and experience a connection to the sacred source. When we return to the sacred source where we truly belong, we feel completely secure, balanced, and fulfilled simply being in the moment. Our energy is recharged, and we are filled with love and wisdom. Let the joy of creative thinking be shared with others and spread happiness. Count your blessings one by one and appreciate every moment. To attain this state-of-being, we must practice meditation. Meditation infuses us with this great joy when we trust our spiritual guides and release attachments to the mind and body.

# 26

## Overcome all partings through the truth

When we lose something that we perceive is a part of ourselves, we feel despair and loneliness. Because we sometimes think that this possession makes us whole, we unknowingly continue to seek it out. When we lose a family member, we experience grief because we took it for granted that we would always have a bond with that person. We perceive these connections as everlasting.

People pass away because of their karma. Their role in this life has simply concluded; their physical life has come to an end. They then return to the place from which they originally came. Thus, instead of grieving when we lose a loved one, we should pray with compassion and warmth for the repose of their soul. When it is time to part ways, strive to experience truth rather than dwell in sadness at the level of the mind. Enrich your understanding of the inner self. We will experience more fulfillment if we strive to understand the truth and pray for the happiness of these departed souls in moments of passing, rather than mourning at the level of the mind.

## 27

## Do good things without expecting a reward

When you consciously wish for the happiness of others with universal love, you do the right thing without expecting a reward in return. Sometimes though we only give importance to our own gain or accomplishments. We exclude others and lose our sense of humanity. One reason for these self-directed motivations is a desire to improve ourselves, but another reason is rooted in a sense of insecurity and self-defense: we lose sight of our own actions because the mind is self-defensive. Overdressing or putting too much emphasis on physical appearance is also a form of self-defense. Karma drives our actions as well as the mind. Doing good things that are motivated by the mind will only feed the ego, because the mind/ego wants praise.

Once we realize this and start meditating on our journey to the truth, we begin to take right actions naturally. We consciously wish for the happiness of others with universal love do the right thing without expecting a reward in return. This is because your actions are neutral—neither good nor bad. You are in the center. Meditation is also neither good nor bad, neither right nor wrong. It is about being in the present moment, in the Now.

**Relax your mind and experience peace:**
Encounter infinite stillness and profound love.
Radiate light like the sun.

The mind experiences a variety of feelings and emotions in life: delight, anger, sorrow, pleasure, pain, loneliness, insecurity, and so on. For this reason the mind vacillates, reacting to diverse events and encounters.

What is behind the vacillating mind? External things don't sway the mind; it is the mind itself. The mind stores past life memories and desires, driving the ego in its incessant demands. Always reactive, the ego-mind is like the ocean, constantly in motion, rising and cresting. It compels the mind to fixate on various attachments. Never satisfied, the ego is stuck in this repetitive cycle.

You might equate the word *ego* with the word *selfish* or a self-obsessive

state of mind, but its underlying meaning actually concerns a consciousness of the "self"—or what we refer to as "me" or "I." Our egos become defensive out of fear, which in turn creates a mindset that perpetuates fear. We unconsciously assume that our ego-mind is who we are on a fundamental level. It is certainly useful in certain aspects of our lives, but it is not our true essence.

Just as there is absolute stillness deep under the surface of the raging sea, so too is there a calm inner sanctum of love and wisdom deep within each of us. The source of all creation, infinite life energy, and divine force resides in these depths. Just as the sun nurtures life on earth, we too are nurtured by the source of creation that gives life to all of humanity.

Let us transcend the ego's longing for external ful-fillment and pay attention to that inner sanctum. Let us cultivate gratitude and unconditional love so that we can live more peaceful, unbiased, balanced lives. By releasing ourselves from the vice grip of the ego, we are able to encounter the truth, become one with God, and shine with grace and radiant abundance like the sun.

# 28

## Everything is your training

People feel like they are playing a thankless role at work when they are given jobs that others have failed to do or did not complete. However, we must accept what is happening around us and view everything as an opportunity for growth. This training is exclusively for you and no one else. We get out of every effort what we put into it. We learn through these efforts, which, in turn, empower us to handle any situation.

Without comparing yourself to others, do everything steadily and with joy. People around you will respond in kind and help you. When you change, others change. You can even leave your job to others with a wish for their success and growth. Sharing work with others also relaxes us. When we respect and appreciate others, we establish good relationships with people, who in turn are also willing to help us. Nurturing the growth of others around us enhances our own growth and our relationships.

# 29

## You don't need to be an honors student in life

Being an honors student is a positive attribute, but sometimes you may be trying hard to be perfect, fearing failure. That said, learning comes with failure, so don't be afraid of it. If you fail and blame yourself—if you chastise yourself for carelessness or inadequacy—you do not learn. Instead of blaming yourself and stagnating, strive to be creative, enjoy the process even more, and produce something from that failure. For example, when you lose your wallet, instead of cursing your bad luck, think positively about what might happen to it. This is a chance to express sympathetic joy. Failure is an opportunity. Oversights are opportunities to learn and change our frame of mind.

It is difficult to get close to a perfect person. People who have known failure are generally more emphatic, understanding, and thoughtful. They are broad-minded and more accessible to people. Failure is an opportunity to become a more expansive person.

# 30

## Know your spiritual guide as a caring mother

We suffer when we are enslaved by our minds. Let us be less connected to the mind and more connected to universal love and to God, the sacred source of existence. This will release us from suffering. Suffering exists when we are disconnected from this sacred source.

Everyone needs help evolving toward this higher state of consciousness. This is a basic truism. In order to improve at golf, for example, you need a good teacher, a high-performance golf club, and good technique. Learning to improve your game on your own without this help would take an extremely long time. Just as we all need people with higher knowledge to help us in our daily aspirations, so too do we need people who can show us the way to the sacred source. Only an enlightened master or spiritual guide—one who becomes a bridge and instructor for your soul—can take you there. The easiest way to reach this enlightened place is to trust your spiritual teacher. When you trust, you flip a switch that activates abundant good energy. You are instantly connected to the sacred source.

# 31

## Appreciate others instead of trying to change them

We tend to notice other people's mistakes and judge them. Meanwhile, we believe that our own way of thinking is the only way to think. This judgmental energy is felt by others and makes them uncomfortable. Even if we remain silent, people will not feel accepted by us. We might give advice or otherwise try to be helpful, but because of this judgmental energy, people won't accept our input with an open mind.

To be receptive to other people and understand them, we must first observe ourselves. The people you want to change are the same people who will change you. Being self-aware will relax others and put their minds at ease, which facilitates change.

Expand your love. Love yourself and be easy on yourself. This is the path to your True Self. Love and wisdom will emerge as well as an understanding of others that will expedite their change.

# 32

## You suffer because you are protected

You are feeling pain now because you are at a turning point. You are about to grow in fundamental ways. You have been given an opportunity to love, forgive, relax, and observe yourself.

We are protected by the greater existence of the sacred source. Without pain, we forget our connection to this sacred source. Pain allows us to remember that we are connected to this source. Thus, we should appreciate our pain.

Now is the time to express gratitude to our mind and body, which may not have felt pain up until now, despite all we have gone through. Experiencing appreciation this way will help us feel greater love, observe ourselves more objectively, deepen our awareness, and protect our mind and body more consciously. We will then approach our true essence, which is connected to eternal life, and experience support from the sacred source.

## 33

# Give thanks regardless how small your role

We tend to envy others. When our co-workers have a more important job, we feel diminished. That said, it is possible that our co-workers are suffering or experiencing any number of unseen emotions. Only when we learn, grow, and have diverse experiences ourselves are we able to evolve in the workplace.

No matter how small the task, we should experience gratitude for what is given to us. Everything comes our way for a reason. Appreciate what is given to you and face it with love. Therein lies a very important lesson. We can purify a negative mindset this way and practice receiving genuine positive energy. Energy stagnates when we are stuck in a negative mindset. Appreciate everything and let the energy flow. Negative energy will then be sublimated and disappear.

# 34

## Purify yourself

When people hear directives or commands, such as "do this" and "do that," they experience resistance. Their egos will resist advice, no matter how good it might be. People may even resist loving words from someone they trust if messages are communicated at the level of ego. If we are too persistent, people will perceive us as meddlesome even if we convey messages out of true love.

Trying to change others is futile. People must come to an awareness themselves in order to change. By the same token, if we change and purify ourselves, others will be influenced by our peaceful energy and start changing at a deeper level. When people are on the same wavelength in relationships, they get along better. Be patient. Purify yourself so that you can help others. People gravitate toward others who radiate positive energy.

# 35

## Forgive everything

Nobody is perfect. We all get angry, envious, blame ourselves, or act selfishly at times. Meditation awakens us on a deep inner level and expedites purification. When we meditate, accumulated ideas and thoughts that may have protected us in the past come to mind and dissipate. At the same time, we become aware of the mechanism of the mind.

We struggle as best we can to live in the darkness, separated from the sacred source of our existence. Our mind is attached and habituated to thought patterns that are hard to release. However, have faith in the process of purifying the mind. Acknowledge the pain of struggling to see the light, express and experience gratitude, and accept everything.

We awaken our divine nature by connecting to the bridge of the source of existence this way. We are then not swayed by the mind and are able to effortlessly understand ourselves and the world at large. Only in this way can we move from darkness to the light, from ignorance to awareness.

# 36

## Empty your mind and your dreams will manifest

The mind creates agony. How can we become a person who is not influenced by the mind? Can we release agony yet control the mind?

Our awareness often stays at the conscious level. On a deeper level, our subconscious stores past experiences and knowledge. On an even deeper level, pure consciousness is directed from the sacred source. There is limited value in memories of past experiences that reside in our subconscious. Thinking on this level is generally self-defeating. We are prone to think "I can't do this" or "what's the use?" This way of thinking drags us down and prevents us from manifesting our dreams. We often believe that we are our minds and are therefore at the mercy of our minds.

To manifest our dreams, we must be aware of the truth and nurture a connection to the sacred source. When we purify and empty our minds, the universe responds and empowers us to manifest our dreams.

## 37

Nurturing your True Self releases an
anti-aging elixir

When we are young, we are effortlessly radiant. As we age, this radiance dissipates. This is because radiance is bound up in external factors, like youth and fashion. No matter how old we are, however, we can still become more vibrant and radiate love and wisdom as we embark on the journey to become our True Self. While external beauty eventually fades, we can refine our mind and body on a deep level, where vibrancy radiates from the soul. This naturally imbues us with a youthful spirit and attitude.

We don't need hormones or collagen to keep our vital energy. We can tap into it and cultivate it from within. We can live a powerful life of joy and gratitude beyond the constraints of time and age.

# 38

## Harmonize with the laws of the universe

People who enjoy what they do tend to take good care of themselves. Feeling good about what you do is paramount. Let us strive to do work that brings us joy and express this joy to others. This feeling, which is for the mutual benefit of everyone around us, gratifies the soul and exalts life. When you bring joy to others as well as to yourself, you cultivate a spirit of cooperation. You then work in harmony with the laws of the universe.

We cannot live alone. We are here to help, support, and give life to others. We cannot work productively in life at work or at play if we are physically unhealthy. Our state of mind affects our physical body as well. When the mind is sick, the body eventually becomes sick. We no longer enjoy life. When we engage in unproductive thoughts—questioning the usefulness of our own actions or the pleasure we derive from them—we diminish ourselves. Judgmental thinking limits possibility, exhausts and weakens our vital energy, and eventually affects everyone around us.

# 39

## When we act with gratitude judgment dissolves

Sometimes the very thing we need in order to grow and evolve is the thing we dislike and avoid the most. It is that simple. We need a foundation on which to build a house. Just as the invisible foundation of a house is firm and solid, so too must we enrich and cultivate the foundation of our inner invisible selves. All great things are built with a certain simplicity which is not seen from the outside. Prosperity is built on simplicity.

We can learn from what we dislike. Aversions give us willpower and wisdom and help us evolve as human beings who appreciate and enjoy life. When we realize that our aversions are invaluable lessons for learning and growth, we are able to evolve and change. When we deepen our awareness and act with gratitude, the polarities of what we like and dislike will disappear. We will be able to express gratitude for everything. We will experience a harmonious way of being, which makes us—and everyone around us—feel comfortable and complete.

# 40

## To lose is to win

Do you ask things of your spouse, partner or family members and end up fighting if they don't respond in your favor? Do you want them to express more love or be more proactive? Being stubborn or hurting others leads nowhere. Expressing forgiveness with a simple "I'm sorry" can immediately transform a strained and uncomfortable situation. It has power. An honest apology is a victory. To lose is to win.

Do not expect too much from or depend too much on your partner. Instead, observe yourself. Express gratitude and deepen your awareness. Express gratitude even to those who are your opponents. You can't fight alone. Appreciate more. Family life often brings out the karma of complaints and anger, but this also helps you clear away karma. Express love and gratitude to your partner for a relationship that honors your true intentions. Respect and appreciation are necessary between family and close friends. Change will follow suit.

## 41

## Children are gifts from the universe

Parents are usually benevolent toward their children and protect them with their lives, though they also get irritated by their behavior. That is because children reveal back to us what we need in order to grow.

Children choose us from the cosmos and enter our wombs that we may foster love, practice forgiveness, learn, understand and purify our karma—and grow. When we are aggressive and reactive with young beings who are pure and don't understand our actions, we generate stress and emotional clutter. Laughter and love are an antidote. We must first love ourselves and then our children. We must respect ourselves as well as the individual personality of each child. Let us look inside ourselves to cultivate compassionate understanding and have gratitude for the existence of the truth.

# 42

## Foster dispassionate love to forestall nosey parents

Parents are frustrating when they are intrusive, but their behavior in fact is an expression of their unconditional love. They want us to succeed. They want us to be capable in life. They want us to excel at school and be healthy. Parents often project their own desires onto their children because they desperately want them to grow up to become good, solid individuals. Some parents grow up with a mandate from their own parents not to make mistakes or trouble others, and so they are groomed to do everything with the utmost conviction.

Often when they are not happy with their own lives, they want with even more fervor for their children to have fulfilling lives. It might seem as if they are trying selfishly to oversee and manage their children's lives, but, in fact, it is often an innocent expression of the degree to which they love and care about them.

In order to have a fulfilling relationship with your parents based on mutual understanding, it is essential to nurture a sense of gratitude and dispassionate love. As their children, we need to accept our parents' love and express appreciation. At the same time, we foster the ability to disengage and cultivate a detached style of love that brings happiness to ourselves and to our parents.

## 43

## Let radiance emanate around you

Perhaps you recall a time when you unintentionally exaggerated, were immodest, or arrogant in public. Perhaps you even engage in this kind of behavior often, even though you are objectively aware of doing so. Sometimes we engage in this kind of behavior because we feel compelled by our competitive society to seek external gratification and approval from others. Even so, because everyone has a different set of values, we often do not feel a sense of true ease or satisfaction if we try to be properly appreciated by those around us.

Instead of seeking satisfaction outside ourselves in this way, we can commit to loving and uplifting ourselves. When we fulfill ourselves on an inner level, we gradually start to cultivate and radiate our own brilliance. To expedite this process, we need to understand both the invisible inner world that resides within and the nature of the mind. We also need to try to become more discerning about and detached from our desires. When we cultivate ourselves in this way, our inner brilliance naturally radiates.

# 44

## Feel love

In order to feel love, we must clear the clutter from our minds. Love doesn't flow in without clear channels of receptivity. When we are stuck in the ego-self, true love doesn't flow in. Only when we release ourselves from the clutch of the ego and become empty will true love flow.

However, many of us have messy lives and are unable to feel love. When we connect to a master or enlightened spiritual guide, the disarray in our lives dissipates and we are prepared to receive love.

People in India are deeply devout and thus receive abundant grace. It is important that we try hard to forge a spiritual path on our own, without any expectations. However, because they have trained and connected to the sacred, a master or spiritual guide can serve as a bridge to help us purify and connect more quickly to essential love.

We must feel that essential love at all costs.

# 45

## Wait while we offer

Modern life is saturated with information. We are quickly exhausted from overusing our senses and our minds. When we awaken our consciousness by purifying our senses and minds, we are able to detach. This is part of the evolution of consciousness: to have true awareness and be capable of simply observing with detachment.

When we use our minds or our senses unconsciously, we develop energetic patterns that automatically play out. To deepen our awareness and transcend our minds, we need to have faith in a master or spiritual teacher who can guide us. We need to remain centered and not use our minds or our senses in a profligate manner. True meditation happens when we prepare our inner landscape this way. Meditation involves doing nothing. We must wait for meditation to happen. When it does, we experience silence and we reconnect to a deep, pristine sense of self. When we wait patiently and are of service in the world, good things happen naturally and synergistically.

Similarly, in relationships we should not ask for things but offer them instead, exercise patience, and simply wait. Abundance will spring forth from deep within and positive, fulfilling relationships will flourish.

# 46

## Focus on everlasting brilliance

As we all know, anything can happen at any moment: a big earthquake or any other catastrophe. Material wealth that has been built up over years or centuries can instantly vanish. We therefore need to transcend the ego-centered self that focuses simply on temporal, material gain and instead cultivate love, peace, forgiveness, and trust in an enlightened spiritual guide. We need to focus not on ephemeral beauty but on everlasting brilliance.

Trusting people are beautiful. If we develop a compliant, loving mind that puts people at ease, things come our way like bees to beautiful flowers. Support comes our way in the form of people and positive opportunities. Instead of seeking external gratification with our ego-centered minds, let us build internal strength through trust.

# 47

## Balance

When our energy is muddled or blocked, we become worn-out, inconsiderate, or insensitive to situations. We unconsciously and automatically take action as a means of self-defense, often with the assumption that what we are doing is for the best. Once we have a negative experience, we tend to avoid similar experiences even though they might be important or beneficial for us. When we experience fear, we tend to shut our eyes and are unable to see things objectively. Karma can compel us to make habitual choices, which result in lack of balance from doing too much or too little.

When we practice teachings that lead to the truth, our mind becomes purified and balanced. As a result, we attain a certain equilibrium: we must be neither too assertive nor too withdrawn. With balance, our intuition sharpens, our wisdom deepens, and we are better equipped to make good choices. When our consciousness evolves, we are able to be as we are. We are empowered with courage and can see objectively and with more clarity. We connect to the source of life instead of connecting to fear, confusion, or other ego-centric emotions. When we choose love and gratitude, we are able to live naturally and with more ease.

# 48

## How to invite the truly precious things

When we connect to the sacred source or the essence of love, we are completely fulfilled. Our need for materialistic gain and egocentric gratification dissipates. But because we are still human, these needs persist. Thus, though we may know intellectually that money is not the most important thing in life, we can't help but focus on it. We need it to buy food, shelter, and other physical necessities. Nevertheless, we might still use our money in unproductive ways. Even with material abundance, we might still be wasteful or buy more things than we truly need. Look around your own home and ask yourself: How many things do I really, truly need? What am I using to its maximum potential?

When we release the power of money, which so captivates the ego, and dedicate our most precious things to a higher place, we get closer to the truth and receive powerful blessings. We open the door for more positive things in our life. Truly precious things in life come our way. Miracles might even occur: relationships improve naturally and those suffering from illness get healthy.

# 49

## Love and gratitude dissolve ill feelings

No matter how many times we hear the word *gratitude*, it is not always easy to readily express it. It is often necessary to first release negative feelings, like regret, before we may experience gratitude. There are also visible and invisible levels of gratitude.

When you look at life with a positive attitude, your body and mind are filled with radiant energy and love. On the other hand, if you look at the world in a negative light, ill feelings persist and smolder within, and you repeat the same cycle. Feelings are converted into anger, doubt, and inconsistency. These feelings continue to smolder until we release them by practicing forgiveness and gratitude. Once we do so, we are able to transcend both the body and mind—and to change.

# 50

## When bad things happen instantly give thanks

When we are provoked by someone, we often fight back. When someone makes cynical remarks, we often respond in kind with twice as much sarcasm. When we experience something unpleasant, we automatically get reactive and aggressive. These reactive responses are often the result of living in a competitive society. We don't want to lose. Men are particularly susceptible to these pressures. In any case, we often think it is better to react to the other party so as to gain a competitive advantage or edge over them. Many of us cannot stop striking back even though we know it is not positive and can even backfire.

Thus, when we experience something unpleasant, it is important to say "thank you" mentally without hesitation. Rather than volley back negative thoughts, look inside yourself. Is there anything you did that may have provoked negativity on the part of the other party? Do you unconsciously judge others? Do you have an unfriendly attitude? The reason things don't always go well often resides within yourself.

# 51

## Cry like a baby

When we become adults, we put pressure on ourselves to be perfect and conduct ourselves appropriately in life. As a result, it is difficult for many of us to let go and cry in front of people.

Even when you want to cry out, do you often stay quiet and swallow your words? Why do babies cry at the top of their lungs simply when they want milk? It is an amazing breathing technique—adults should try it once in a while. After crying like a baby, you will experience great tranquility.

Babies don't breathe inside the womb. Their hearts beat and their breathing is suspended while they are connected to their mothers through the umbilical cord. Babies gradually acquire normal breathing by crying out, which trains their lungs. They master normal, quiet breathing as they grow. Sometimes crying out like a baby, no matter what your age, can alleviate pain and promote serenity.

# 52

## Awareness brings incredible abundance

Instead of trying to learn a little through a lot of different people, strive for self-realization. Self-realization is a true pleasure. Self-realization is happiness. It enriches you. With the guidance of a master or spiritual guide, go forth on your journey toward the light.

When we start to practice meditation, we become aware of many things. Eventually, everything merges into the sacred source. When we return to our True Selves, karma, which has been created by the mind, rises to the surface to be released. Our values change, and we become aware of the burdens we carry. Awareness fosters further awareness.

However, those of us who tend to think in a negative fashion might find that thoughts which emerge through meditation are painful. That is why it is imperative to have a master or spiritual guide when we practice meditation. Tremendous memories dwell in our subconscious. In order to enter and purify the subconscious, we need a spiritual guide who has attained enlightenment.

# 53

## Free from your limited consciousness

Many of us are separated from the sacred source and live with a limited state of consciousness. When we meditate, we are able to encounter our divine essence, the True Self. Meet your True Self in deep meditation and be free from the constraints of your limited consciousness.

To that end, it is important for us to work with an enlightened meditation teacher or guide. We need a good coach or teacher when we engage in sports or the arts. The same is true on the path to the truth.

Let us not practice simple meditation but commit to meditation that is focused on the truth. This is the best way to quickly establish a strong conduit for receiving vital energy. Sometimes it is difficult to give this our best effort, but it is important to try with our hearts to stay committed and avoid the distractions of daily life that make us lose sight of the truth. When you work with an enlightened spiritual guide, you receive energy from a higher dimension and can purify yourself on a deep level.

# 54

## Sating the ego is not true healing

To achieve emotional balance and dispel negative feelings like sadness and anger, we sometimes try too hard to be positive and happy, or we may deceive ourselves by behaving kindly to others. However, this can eventually exhaust us since the process is all-consuming. When done at the level of the mind, it simply strengthens the ego. This might bring momentary fulfillment but does not justify the ego and is not true healing. Filling sorrow with joy is ephemeral. Compensating sadness with happiness, the ego is sated, but we are not healed.

Negative feelings emerge when the ego-mind blames unfulfilled feelings for experiences we have had in the past. We are often unaware of this because we are ignorant. When certain events trigger the same negative emotions as we experienced in the past, it is an opportunity to heal those negative emotions. Let us release the ego-mind and return to the pure mind. Let us connect to the True Self, which is the essence of love, and release negative emotions. This is true healing.

**When the mind softens, we see the beauty of compliance:**
True compliance involves trusting your True Self.

Being compliant and following the advice of a coach or teacher is the quickest way to advance and acquire knowledge or skills in academics, sports, or the arts. Reluctance, however, can make this difficult. We are all sometimes stubborn in relationships, which we often regret later. Despite our deep heartfelt wishes, we also sometimes find it difficult to love humanity. It is greatly liberating to be true to oneself.

We might think that it is naive to blindly comply with authority or be obedient, but the true meaning here involves trusting our True Self and surrendering to it. Many of us trust the ego and assume that the ego-mind is who we are. But it is beyond this false sense of self that we experience the essence of love and wisdom that keeps us alive. This is the soul: The True Self that belongs to the sacred source. It is a form of divinity. We must trust and surrender to it.

This form of divinity is omnipresent, but we often don't notice it because we are fixated by the ego-mind. The ego-mind obscures the truth. How can we ever become truly compliant? We must trust our spiritual guides who have become one with divinity by purifying the body and mind.

We feel close to our spiritual guides because they have physical bodies. They are a bridge to God. We must surrender to them with full, ego-less trust. They are aligned with the same qualities that exist within us, which are reflections of the sacred source, and are thus able to awaken us on a deep level.

# 55

## When you dedicate you become the universe

We will never understand others if we are stubborn and our hearts are closed. Only when we reconcile with people and symbolically or literally shake hands do we feel affirmed and positive. Relationships develop and flourish. We must remove desires, self-defenses, and ego-related impediments in order to become more expansive individuals. When we assert ourselves our egos manifest. However, when we surrender ego and dedicate ourselves to the divine, we become one with the universe.

We may think that the ego is intractable, but it is only an impediment. It is resistant to letting go and surrendering to the vast realm of love that exists in the sacred source. We are an essence which has been separated from the sacred source, God. When the ego surrenders to the sacred source, we merge and become one with this essence, the True Self.

# 56

## Love and believe the souls of others

In all relationships, the ego reacts in anger to personal provocations or danger. Conflicts are always at the level of ego. But the ego is neither your True Self nor the True Self of others.

Great love in the cosmos fosters life. Our lives are endowed with learning opportunities. All of us are children of God and connected to each other. Believe in and love the soul of others. Since we are an essence that has been separated from the sacred source—God—we perceive God in others, who are here to teach us. As a messenger of God, they are trying to help us become aware of our egos so that we can purify them.

Emotions caused by the reactive ego are important learning opportunities. We must appreciate others. We must believe in and respect their pure inner essence and not judge outward appearances. Everyone we meet creates an opportunity to learn. Believe in others and love them by praying for their happiness.

# 57

## We are created through love in the cosmos

Our existence is a speck on this earth, which itself is a small planet in the universe. From the perspective of the macrocosm, we are a mere grain of sand. That said, our body is composed of the same materials as the cosmos. Thus, our body is also the cosmos. We are tiny, and yet we are the essence of love in the universe.

The wisdom of God works within our body, fills us with vital energy and love, and fuels life. Our existence is created through love in the cosmos.

We live with much worry on this earth. Our anxieties are part of our growth and purification. They are learning opportunities that endow us with greater awareness and help us evolve toward the essence of love.

Remember that the pure love that resides in the universe requires no payback. If you cultivate that love, you will be able to return to the original sacred essence and experience boundless tranquility and happiness.

# 58

## Entrust everything to God

Messages from the universe exist everywhere in our daily lives, but we don't always notice them.

The ego, our insecurities, and personal desires prevent us from strengthening our belief in ourselves. We must release these preoccupations and entrust everything to God. We must focus on the essence of the sacred source that brought us here. Love exists in the essence of the sacred source. When we release the ego, infinite love appears, and we receive true messages.

If you tune into what seems to be limitless love from the source through your ego, things may appear to go well in the beginning, but messages will ultimately be confusing. Messages at the level of the ego will control you. Your consciousness will feel separate and your life energy might be wasted or misspent. It is essential to maintain an enlightened state of consciousness. Follow the guidance of a master or spiritual teacher who understands the development of the inner self.

# 59

## The balance of the cosmos

The universe creates various recurring natural disasters in order to restore balance. We human beings are composed of a mind, body, and soul. We are thus the embodiment of a microcosm within the macrocosm. Negative behavior, words, and thoughts can destroy harmony in this microcosm and cause conflicts within the mind, body, and soul. Our energy gets off-balance and, as a result, we may get sick or things simply will not go well for us.

This negative energy spreads out to the universe, which tries to reestablish its original, peaceful state of balance. Difficulties and natural upheavals may arise in this process. Troubles arise to endow you with the strength to purify yourself. In their own small way, your actions affect the balance of the cosmos. By enhancing our awareness of these events, we learn and accrue more knowledge.

The cycle of the universe—birth to death—is the same cycle that we experience through purification of the self. We also experience the same cycles as the vast cosmos, evolving and growing little by little in the process.

# 60

## Cells are part of the cosmos

There are countless stars in the vast cosmos. These stars appear and disappear. The creatures on this earth are also born, live, and pass away. Where do they come from and where do they go? The essence of the sacred source makes them appear and disappear. There is not only a visible world; there is also an invisible essence to all things that restores balance.

We human beings have developed our knowledge of space in order to understand the universe. We have developed various sciences to attempt to understand the origin of this world as well. Science however cannot find the truth. It can never find God or determine where we come from, because human beings, born from the essence of the sacred source, are created by God. We are born and we pass away. This cycle has always been shrouded in mystery.

The mind, body, and soul are part of the cosmos. So too are our cells, which are the subtle essence within the body and mind. Though we cannot reach the origin of the vast universe, as microcosms of the universe we can access transcendent knowledge and attain enlightenment through the journey to Samadhi, the practical journey to the inner self.

# 61

## Beyond the most advanced science access the immeasurable

Within the atom, the smallest unit of all material, there exists the nucleus, electrons and neutrons. They are all perfectly balanced. They are further divided into elementary particles, which vibrate. This has been confirmed by quantum physics, the latest and most advanced field of science that works with the smallest of materials. This leading science measures things in infinitesimal numbers. Human beings are composed of these same materials that exist in the universe.

An immeasurable and mysterious world exists in the universe, beyond the understanding of the most advanced science. Surprisingly, more than five thousand years ago, Himalayan Masters knew every detail about the smallest materials. They were able to access the world beyond these materials and hold sway over them. Through ascetic training they gained access to this immeasurable world, found what the smallest materials are composed of, transcended them, and attained the ultimate Samadhi (enlightenment). Through this process they encountered God, the essence of the sacred source, and were liberated from mind and body.

# 62

## The invisible and profound truth of the universe becomes truly visible

What is consciousness? What is God? What is the mind? What is the body? What is the pursuit of the truth? The science of Samadhi involves understanding oneness on an experiential level. This is the essence of the sacred source which creates the mind and body. In Samadhi we shift into a momentary state of consciousness beyond time and space. We human beings are not in touch with the True Self that lies within the mind and body. We live with limited consciousness. The truth of the universe is invisible and so profound that we cannot comprehend it. Ordinary people are unaware of this truth. Thus, we live with suffering. We are unaware of our connection to the essence of the sacred source and are swayed by events and people as they come and go in our daily lives.

The ultimate truth is that all living creatures are made to live with the blessing and grace of the universe. A master or enlightened spiritual guide can bestow this grace, Anugraha, to others. The blessing of Anugraha penetrates deep within like a laser and transforms and regenerates the body and mind. It evokes peace, love, and empowerment.

# 63

## Cultivate true wisdom

In order to live in good health and happiness in this world, we must make the right choices. Our mind and our senses must work properly and in harmony. To this end, the true self supports the body and mind from deep within the soul. When you transcend the True Self, you are in touch with the essence of the sacred source. The essence of the sacred source is transcendental, but a troubled, anxious mind and body impedes us from experiencing it. When our minds and bodies become clear and open by releasing this anxiety through meditation, we experience deep tranquility and become one with our True Self. Once we experience this, we are always filled with peace and love. We live on a daily basis with a serene, nonjudgmental mind. When you become more profoundly aware of the world around you, you live with more creativity and inspiration.

When we view the world on an intuitive level, beyond the senses and from deep within, we understand things in their totality. We grasp the whole picture. True wisdom comes to us through this intuition and empowers us to live inspirationally in the world at large.

# 64

## Know all

Our journey starts within as we seek the truth and encounter our True Self. We awaken and purify ourselves on an invisible level through meditation of sound and light, galvanizing subtle, inner energies that transform us. As a result, we are transformed: our attachments disappear, our understanding deepens, and we are able to move into a deeper state. Through the grace of Anugraha, we eventually meet the True Self and become one with the essence of the sacred source. This is magnificent.

Our mind and body are the universe. They are a microcosm of the same universe that lies above. Eventually, we understand these things on a deep level and have a far-reaching perspective on life. When you experience profound meditation and understand the true nature of your mind and body, you will understand everything, even the afterlife. We understand not only how our bodies function—our eyes, our ears, all of our senses—but also a range of phenomena, from physiology, psychology, economic sciences, and political sciences, to cytology, atomic energy, spirituality, cosmology, the evolution of souls, and the afterlife.

# 65

## Everything is a process of purification

Even though you may strive toward a goal and work hard, your mind might be distracted with thoughts. Without the power of concentration, the mind unconsciously fixates on things, judgments, and worries. When you practice meditation with a master or spiritual guide, you experience concentration and the willpower to persevere. Part of this practice involves the vibration of a holy sound, or a mantra. What is happening now is part of the process of purification.

At the beginning of your meditation practice, distracting thoughts wander through your mind. This, however, is the process of purification. Appreciate everything as a gift—as part of the purification and the path toward the truth. It is important to accept everything with trust and faith and keep practicing meditation. The mind is very stubborn and strong and does not relent. Your mind and body will become still when you are guided into deep meditation with God's grace. That said, the activity of the mind is proof that you are alive. Therefore, when your mind is active, consider it from a broader perspective and think to yourself: "I am alive."

# 66

## People evolve over an immense period of time

Yagya (or yajna) is a purification fire ceremony performed in India. When enlightened masters conduct a Yagya, various wishes are sent into the universe through the power of prayer, fire, and profound faith. These wishes are then realized through the transformative energy of fire.

This energy of fire exists within us. Himalayan Masters know how to control and manipulate vital energy called *prana*, strengthening it to create this energy of fire. They use it to burn the bad karma of the mind and body, transforming both in the process. This is conducted through a powerful process called Anugraha Kriya.

Normally, people evolve through the never-ending cycle of life and death. You return to the Great Cosmos on a journey that transpires over an immense period of time. Himalayan Masters can perform miracles by expeditiously purifying, transforming, and evolving your mind, body, and soul. When you receive the blessing of Anugraha Kriya, you will immediately be transformed, experience deep tranquility, and return to the essence of the sacred source—the universe of great love.

# 67

## Balance the five energies

Our body is said to be a microcosm of the universe and to share the same elements. Our physical bodies contain the same elements as the universe and share the same principles of balance. All five elements of the universe exist in our bodies: earth, water, fire, wind, and space. As the universe exists in balance, so too does our body seek balance. When energies gravitate toward one another and veer off-balance, we lose balance as well and get sick.

For example, when physical or mental fatigue causes you to lose balance, you become sensitive to wind energy and are susceptible to catching a cold. You feel cold when you fray your nerves and exhaust your energy. This is because the element of fire is depleted. To accelerate your metabolism and rejuvenate yourself, it is better to burn the fire energy of the stomach. Your body connects deeply to the elements of the universe this way. Himalayan wisdom is based on the five energies of the universe. It awakens, purifies, and strengthens these energies through meditation. By harnessing the power of nature, you can live freely.

# 68

## Respond with love

We have incarnated over multiple lives and our souls continue to progress. Karma is the result of our actions that have settled into fixed values. By awakening the inner self, we recognize these values. By releasing them, we can return to the sacred source.

Since the mind is always working, we often think that the mind is our True Self. When something happens, the mind reacts through the filter of its values. When you continue to do good deeds, awaken the inner self, and purify your karma, you understand these intrinsic values and how they are expressed. You can ultimately transcend them and transform them into love. Let us try to accrue good karma and respond to everything with love. Only then will we experience inner peace, which will help us manifest peace in the world. This is because our state of mind is reflected in this world. When you respond with love, without imposing values or judgment, peace will come to you.

May you and everything around you be peaceful!

# 69

## Surrender to the flow

We often have the illusion that we live by ourselves, but the truth is that we are made to live in balance with the cosmos. Therefore, it is good to relax and leave everything to the natural flow of life. Everything flows well and is naturally guided, not by you, but by an infinite power.

When we put pressure on our minds to do everything ourselves, our energy does not flow smoothly. Instead, it creates stress. Everything is a learning opportunity provided by an unseen, greater power. If we surrender to this higher power and become a vessel for it, we will experience enjoyment every moment.

# 70

## Purify the inner self and transcend it

Most of us desperately seek wealth and happiness. We work hard in the belief that we will obtain good things. And yet even if we work hard and acquire things, we often still experience problems when we are not aligned with the truth of the universe. Since we are often unaware of this, we work hard and try to affirm ourselves. In fact, many of us have worked hard and done very well in life. However, are we in fact happy with our way of life? What if there were a way of life that was easier and flowed more seamlessly?

When we work hard but things don't go well, it is often because we are relying too much on the life of the mind. We suffer as a result. The true way of life is to purify the inner self and transcend it. When we have problems, we should consider them learning opportunities. For that to happen, we must trust and connect to a higher-dimensional energy and reinforce our positive energy. When we are endowed with power from the divine source, we are empowered with the vital energy and wisdom we need to surmount any problem that comes our way.

# 71

## Radiate good energy

Some people are perceived as angry even when they are not angry. This has to do with the type of energy they release. Even though they are not angry in the present moment, they were angry in the past and that vibration is engrained in them. For this reason, many people don't know how they are perceived by others, or what kind of energy they create and release. We might take care of our outward appearance, but what about our minds?

Are we truly free to get angry or sad simply because our mind compels us to feel this way? Do we not create trouble when we do whatever we want? Our state of mind transmits a vibration that affects people around us. When our mind suffers, people around us receive the vibration of suffering. When we are happy, we radiate good energy that makes people around us happy. We must cultivate this awareness and be free from this cycle. We must send good vibrations and happiness to ourselves and those around us.

# 72

## Restore our intrinsic nature

We live on this earth in a solar system in a galaxy that is part of an infinite universe. Therefore, we are part of the cosmos. As children of nature, we are an intrinsic part of nature. Everything exists according to the laws of nature, and the great power of nature exists within us. We are unaware of this, however, and our inner self is often confused with various desires that disconnect us from this intrinsic part of our nature.

Nature always tries to maintain harmony. Disasters and global warming occur to rebalance the earth. Similarly, when we lose the balance of our body, we experience worry and anxiety. We often suffer and get sick before we try to restore balance. This is a learning process and an aspect of true wisdom that we do not learn in school.

Let us restore our intrinsic nature by purifying ourselves deeply many times over, expanding awareness, releasing unnecessary things, and returning to an original state of grace. In so doing, our bodies will stay healthy and our minds will be stress-free.

## 73

### Awaken the pure nature within

Nature relaxes us. Its energy, which exists all around us—from beautiful mountain vistas, glimmering seas, and bountiful streams, to the smell of the earth and the breeze on our skin—calms and energizes us. There is also power in it. When you awaken the pure nature within yourself, your inner light starts to shine.

Nature and the universe exist within us: the sun, the moon, and water. By purifying our mind and body—by becoming aware of this and refining our senses accordingly—we can awaken and harness the power of nature. Mother earth endows everything with mercy. Water is free and has the power to cleanse. The sun shines light freely onto the earth, creating and nurturing life.

Our body is like the earth: when our mind is obscured by karma, it is like the sun veiled in a haze. Therefore, our bodies lose energy when our minds are murky or cluttered. When these mental obstructions are released, we can encounter the essence of the sacred source. When we return to this sacred source, our minds and bodies are filled with the power of the sun, love, and peace. This is the process of life in which we are all engaged.

# 74

## Release the attachment

True wealth does not come with material abundance. Rather, it comes in maintaining harmony with our own microcosm and regenerating ourselves. We are then in the "now," relaxed, peaceful, and satisfied just as we are. We do not need to fill ourselves up with distractions or receive praise for our work or accomplishments. We are simply fulfilled as we are. We might not always be happy in life, but this is also necessary. It is not a waste. Sickness is not a waste. It is endowed with learning opportunities. We must appreciate this by expressing gratitude.

There is no waste in our lives. Our lives are wonderful. To live is wonderful. Heaven is not a place we go after death. It exists when our minds are transformed in the moment. Everything is wonderful when this happens: the world, you, your life.

# 75

## Release objects, people and experiences

Many people do not understand the word *danshari*. It means to cut out, throw away, release. We arc all attached to various things, some of which we might have a very hard time releasing. But attachment wastes energy because it fosters dependency. Thus, when we let go of various things at home, we feel light. The same is true with the mind: the mind attaches itself not just to objects but also to people and experiences.

Even though releasing attachments of the mind is a process that leads to the True Self, people might feel fear. Where there is desire, there is suffering. This is largely because we are very conscious of material things, and we think that they define us. We believe that the mind is who we are. Thus, we believe that by letting go of the mind, we will let go of who we are. This is not the case, because we simply return to our True Self.

# 76

## True freedom

We are obsessed with various things in our daily lives. If we cling to these things, our anxiety does not dissipate. In fact, we feel tremendous fear—fear of losing a family member, for example, or losing things imbued with great personal value. When we are conscious that we are a soul—when we experience love and are one with God—we do not feel fear because we are completely fulfilled on an entirely different level. However, most of us focus on and believe only in the visible world. Because we operate at the level of the mind, we feel fear.

Even though we may feel safe with our obsessions, they are a heavy burden. They are supposed to make us feel safe, but, in fact, they create situations that generate fear. To be truly free, we must release these things and, in so doing, release ourselves. When we are aware of our obsessions and become our True Self— when we are released from our own enslavement to the mind—we truly relax. True freedom is waiting for you beyond your attachments. Our soul is free, and we are at peace. When you release your obsessions, you naturally give love to others.

# 77

## Become one

When we walk down the road to truth and let go of various obsessions of the mind and body, we become free and merge into a realm of expansive love. We merge into this realm of expansive love like the Himalayan snow melts into water and flows into a stream, which meets the Ganges River. We call this surrender.

Our minds merge into our souls and surrender. We become one with the sacred source of the cosmos, the cradle of our souls. We become one in the same way that a river merges into a sea and, at last, its energy becomes part of that sea. We merge into love and become one.

Although different forms of energy and consciousness can coexist, they eventually merge into one higher consciousness. This is what it means to become One.

# 78

## Listen with an open, compliant mind

When you complain about everything, new things and experiences do not come your way. Children are often free from doubt and objections. They quickly absorb things. Adults often do not have this kind of agility. That's why it is important to empty our minds, put aside our thoughts, and be receptive to good things. This is the case even at school: knowledge is not assimilated if we do not listen to teachers with an open, compliant mind.

Even as we return on our journey to the sacred source, we close the door to the new when our minds are doubtful. Only when we free our minds do we open the door to this journey. Our ego-minds cultivate doubt and hamper our receptivity. We need to make space and take our egos out of the equation in order to have open, compliant minds. You do not have to believe everything on this page. Simply practice the road to the truth using your intuition!

# 79

## Suicide doesn't end suffering

Apparently, more than thirty thousand people a year commit suicide in Japan. Proportionately, this is one of the highest rates of suicide in the world—higher than the annual rate of transportation fatalities. Those who commit suicide have a fundamental misunderstanding that ending their life resolves everything. The ego makes them focus only on the present, not on what happens after death or in the next life. Even if they commit suicide, the mind will not disappear. Its suffering will not end. Ending one's own life based on false judgments of the ego-mind leaves a big scar on the soul.

We come into this world to recognize the truth and return to the sacred source, where we experience the love of the cosmos. We were born to give selfless love while we naturally live out our lives. Our bodies are a gift from God. Let us work hard on what we are given. By learning from the world at large and loving ourselves and others, we cultivate selfless love. In so doing, we exalt life and quite possibly reduce the number of suicides in the world at large.

# 80

## Tune your consciousness to sacred sound

Often the chatter we hear is simply the sound of our own distracting thoughts. Do not pay attention. On the other hand, the holy sound of a mantra that is bestowed on us at a diksha is part of the esoteric teaching of meditation. Let us develop the vibrations of that sound. The power of a mantra purifies all the white noise and chatter of the ego. Its vibrations are also the energy of God and always protect us. Similarly, there is a sound inside us called *nada*, which is also the sound of silence.

The vibrations of a mantra endowed from a master or spiritual guide are mysterious and work differently, depending on the type of vibration at hand. Its sound and energy originate from God, the essence of the sacred source. The vibrations of the holy sound of a mantra have a scientific effect that conditions and purifies the body and mind. It releases toxic thoughts in the mind, restores balance, and transports us to the sacred source beyond the mind. In the source there is the great essence, which is the origin of the cosmos, peace, and love.

**You are the cosmos:**
Return to the pure essence within yourself and the universe. The entire universe exists within and God is our source.

There are myriad galaxies containing countless stars in the universe. The immense universe is finely balanced, wherein birth and death incessantly unfold. Within all this is the solar system and the earth. Humanity on earth is also part of the universe and exists in its balance.

The origin of everything in the universe, including humanity, belongs to the essence of the source of creation. In other words, it is God's creation.

We too have the same elements as the sun, the moon, and the planets. We are comprised of the same elements that form the universe and, as such, we are an embodiment of the universe.

At the beginning of the creation of humanity, the invisible source of creation transmitted prana or life energy, as well as a source of material essence. Together, they gradually shaped our physical form. This is a process called *descending*, in which the invisible void appears first. It is then followed by wind and fire. Thereafter, fire turns to water, water turns to earth, and gradually a visible body is formed.

There are also several invisible layers that form the body: a subtle astral body, and a more subtle causal body, wherein lies the soul. The body can furthermore be divided into seven elements: a physical body, an emotional body, a spiritual body, a mental body, a sound body, a light body, and a conscious body. The mind is part of the mental body and has grown very powerful. It creates desires, which attract mental clutter that obscures the mind. This is the process by which we forget that we are an embodiment of the universe created by God. Our inner self is often in chaos, causing pain, suffering, and impediments that hinder our evolution. If we experience the microcosm within, return to the sacred source, and encounter our True Self through meditation, we achieve a state of completion. This is the evolutionary path of consciousness, a process called *ascending*.

By cleansing and awakening the microcosm obscured by the mind, we discover the mysteries of the universe and the hand of God. Transcending the body and mind is nothing but a return to the essence of the sacred source and our True Self. Be your own master who understands the mechanism of the body and mind and garner the power to balance and harmonize them both.

# 81

## Face life with love

There are many kinds of love. Depending on our karma, each one of us has a different perception of the word *love*. Some of us imagine the love between a man and a woman. Others imagine love from their parents or other people. The love we evoke here is pure love that transcends desire. This love is more immense than personal or attachment love. It is love without the impediment of the ego. It is merciful. It is even beyond mercies as it is universal, everlasting, primordial love.

Love evolves. The attractions and aversions of the ego are eventually purified and transformed into maternal love: undiscriminating, natural, godlike. Universal love comes our way when we empty the mind and awaken the center of our hearts, which are beyond the mind, in order to purify and transcend. We should all strive to live from this place of universal love. Everything goes right when we act with pure love, without the mind's agitations or expectations.

# 82

## Free your heart

Living a life preoccupied by constraint and pretension is burdensome. Even if we have good intentions, they will not last long. Unbeknownst to us, even our kindness might annoy people. Even when we feel we are enjoying our lives, while our ego is in control, we are not experiencing true freedom. Our minds may be content when our desires are met, but our True Selves can never be happy.

When we awaken spiritually and transcend the ego, we become free in a true sense. We may discern if our contentment is from the ego, which compels us to fixate on looking outside ourselves and seeking praise, or if it is from the deep love that resides in our souls. When we move beyond the concept of values and free our hearts, we are relaxed and perceive the world with objectivity and peace. Deep meditation allows us to experience deep love without obsession. This is the path toward loving ourselves and others and ultimately experiencing true freedom.

# 83

## Stay just as you are

What is on your mind? Do you have an obsessive mind that clings to ephemeral pleasures? Are you looking for happiness here and there, trying to fulfill your desires while you experience both happiness and sadness? Where on earth are you heading? Many of us are often so preoccupied with moving forward and doing things that we cannot stay still. We misconstrue the mind as ourselves and are preoccupied with its constant vacillations and attachments. Held captive by our minds, we only know one way of perceiving and feeling.

We are not born with a vacillating mind. Our essential self is transcendent and comes into this world all-knowing. This existence is our birthright and it is stable, fulfilling, and anxiety-free. It does not compel us to always seek new and better things. Everything is within us. The True Self is our real, natural self. Rediscover yourself as the sacred source that fulfills everything.

We can be who we are, here in the moment, without doing anything at all. To know this is the first step to becoming one's own master.

# 84

## Pure essence loves you profoundly

How do you feel about yourself? Do you like or dislike yourself?

How you perceive yourself is not your True Self. Everyone has a True Self within. It is the soul of the source of love, the existence of creation, the sacred source. Your life is sustained by a pure presence that infuses you with profound love. When the mind is clear—when there are no likes or dislikes, when mental clutter disappears—your True Self emerges. However, if your mind is full of anxiety and frustration, you lose your sense of gratitude and become stressed. This is what happens in the world of the mind. In the world of humanity, the source of existence and the True Self seem far away.

To gain access to our True Selves, we must express more gratitude to our True Selves. We must thank our minds, our bodies, and everything around us. We must hold with love and appreciation the existence of our True Selves, which is always sustaining us. In so doing, we connect with love and faith to the presence of the sacred source. This presence imbues us with love and radiance.

# 85

## Realize the priceless

The natural blessings of life exist in our beautiful, perfectly functioning minds and bodies. How many of us are aware of this fact? Are we wasting our ability to relish this truth by lamenting what we don't have? We often ignore the wonderful attributes bestowed upon us and forget to express gratitude. Instead, we waste our vital life energy.

Sometimes we even unconsciously hurt others out of ignorance. We sometimes blame ourselves or hate others in order to survive in our competitive society. Other times we upset people by always demanding things without expressing gratitude. Once we become aware of the pricelessness of what we have already been given, we cannot help but pray for forgiveness for that which we have done through ignorance and arrogance.

Becoming aware of the pricelessness of what we have already been given is the door to enlightenment and the awakening of sacredness.

# 86

## Forgive ourselves to go forward

It is hypocritical to keep blaming ourselves for failures or for hurting others and to believe that we have no right to be loved. We often do this to elicit sympathy. This is done not by us but by our egos. But it is useless to keep blaming ourselves and limit ourselves to values imposed by our egos.

We must forgive ourselves in order to access the power to keep moving forward. From now on, let us develop our consciousness and reflect on this reality in order to move forward in our journey. Let us grow and evolve into people who share and give, instead of being stuck only with demands. Let us use the energy given to us to guide others from darkness to light and not dissipate our energy with guilt. To do this, we must pray. We need its power to forgive ourselves to keep moving forward in life. The great existence that sustains our lives does not judge us. Only our minds and our karma obscure the truth.

# 87

## Cry with all your might

We are always loved and protected, no matter what happened to us in the past. We may overflow with tears because we have encountered through our True Selves something that we have longed for. When we see this light of the truth, we release huge amounts of tension and can finally relax on a deep level. This can provoke abundant tears. We must not hesitate to shed as many tears as we want. Cry more. Cry as much as you can. We must release all the tribulations that have entangled our minds.

From now on, let us live with love that is free from obsession. Let us live with faith. When we have faith in a guide or master who is the bridge between the existence of the sacred source and ourselves, our ability and power to receive is strengthened.

Trust is a way of expressing love. Strong faith generates a flow of good, positive energy. Our negative past, filled as it may be with doubt, worry, and anxiety, will soften and be released. Only then will we believe in not only ourselves but also the great existence that is the sacred source. We will encounter inner truth, which is also the truth of the universe.

# 88

## Accept ourselves as we are

We all feel relaxed with little children. Children do not judge. They always radiate innocent, harmless energy to everyone. The childlike state of being "as we are" is our True Self, though we adults have difficulty being in this state.

By the time we are adults, we have spent a lifetime striving to achieve. We have done many things to fulfill the outside world, such as paying attention to our appearance, social status, etc. We do this even knowing that if we continue on the same path it will eventually exhaust and never fulfill us. We must accept ourselves as we are now. We are okay as we are. We must love our inner selves in order to encounter the deep truth of the universe. We all long for this. Just as a thirsty man craves water in the desert, so too do we crave this connection with the deep truth.

When we encounter our True Self, our soul shines.

# 89

## Honor and treasure the mind and body

To love ourselves is to find truth. It is to find and love the true, essential self within. It is also to respect our mind and body. Instead of treating them with disrespect, we must honor and treasure the mind and body.

We often don't respect or treat ourselves properly. We depend on external realities and are often preoccupied by trivial matters instead of taking care of our True Selves. The more we struggle, the more we cultivate the ego. We miss out on important things, like love and joy and deep connections, because we are not using energy in a natural way.

Love yourself. Respect and take good care of yourself. We must not forget that our existence is always protected and loved. In order to maintain a connection to this protection and love, we need to connect to a master or spiritual teacher who can guide us to the sacred source. In so doing, we are bestowed with love and power. If we believe and leave everything to our master or spiritual guide, we are given abundant grace through the blessing of Anugraha. Eventually, we become enlightened.

# 90

## Let's return to the silence

We are often influenced by our egos and do not really know what we are doing in life. We complain, feel sad, and are confused, confrontational, and swayed by our emotions. It is difficult to manage the mind. When we study and learn, we can't help but judge others and argue. This only takes us away from connecting to our True Selves.

When you connect to your True Self, there are no complaints or excuses. You are immersed in silence and peace. We were born in silence. Let us return there. Everything exists in silence. It is in silence that we remember who we are. The ego softens and is released in silence. There is true purity here. We feel fulfilled and protected simply by being in silence. There is no anxiety here. There is true peace, and we may live in the Here and Now.

# 91

## Love God and the master

There is a way called *Bhakti*, which teaches us to love God and a spiritual guide or master. It is called the way of trust and care, and as we practice it, we do indeed trust more and take better care of ourselves. When we trust a master or spiritual guide and receive and practice a mantra, we are protected by something much bigger than ourselves and feel assured. Our karma is purified, and we quickly feel at ease. Gradually, the love within us develops into pure love, compassion, and universal love. Eventually, we achieve a state of enlightenment.

When we learn the truth and reach the highest state as a human being, we are able to save both ourselves and others. Many of us love variety in our lives and get swayed by it. If we love food, we overeat. If we love our friends, we tend to go astray rather than abide by the truth. But when we love our spiritual guides and practice devotion, we will find the way to the truth. Do not stray from the path of love. Love the real, pure path.

# 92

## The center path is ageless

If we want to excel at anything, we need to start at an early age and practice. Our abilities and our environment are also important. Normally to develop any skill we must practice the same things over and over again, but a more highly evolved way to develop is to transform the quality of our mind, body, and soul.

We all have the power to become enlightened and evolve in this way as human beings. By returning to the source of ourselves, to the truth, we can achieve enlightenment, as well as the power and wisdom to control everything. By adding love to that equation, we have limitless power to manifest our wishes and dreams.

This powerful method of reaching the source of mind and body is the alchemy of Anugraha Kriya, which is also called the "way of energy." No matter who you are or how old you are, you can get closer to the highest state of enlightenment. There is no age limit for this path. The Siddha Master awakens what is called *Sushumna* in Sanksrit, which means the center path of energy. This guides us toward enlightenment. Trust, love, and wisdom unfold within and open our eyes to the light.

# 93

## Share profound love

These days we seem to have forgotten about love. We are always stuck in our heads. In the past, people had faith and were devoted to God. When people of faith drink water from the Ganges river, they are healed of disease. Without faith these same people—those who believe that the river is filthy—will get sick. This is because the mind has the power to color reality.

Our mind and way of thinking have the power to materialize things in our lives. For this reason, we should express love to others with respect and grace. This is possible only through deep love, not the ego's desire to be loved, and through the daily practice of good deeds.

When we begin this inner journey and experience silence in the innermost recesses of the mind, we are eventually able to transcend the mind and access eternal love. This universal love is where we come from and where we belong. We are all destined to return to this place now.

# 94

## Become a leader who personifies love

It is essential that we work on a daily basis to keep the mind and body alive and well. Even if we think we hate our workplace, God has given us an opportunity to learn. We should consider this opportunity a means of evolving in our daily work. Interpersonal stress and other pressures we might experience at work are a purifying expression of the ego that comes from our past karma. Overcoming these stresses and pressures is one way to evolve. When we expand our awareness or capacity to love, people around us are healed and transformed along with us. Express gratitude, focus on your work, and do your best while you encourage those around you.

Everyone tries hard to live. Having a place to work brings happiness. We must try not to obsess about what others think of us or about being loved by everyone. Instead, we should share and express universal love. We achieve universal love through meditation and prayer. When we share this selfless love that is connected to the source, our families and workplaces will change.

We are destined to become leaders in the sharing of love. We have no choice. Let us strive, so that we may change others.

# 95

## Experience love in all

We are truly loved from the source of existence, but we hardly recognize this. We only recognize what we see with our eyes, so we often misunderstand and think that the more delightful things we are given in life, the more we are loved. But it may also be true that when we are given fewer of these gifts, we are, in fact, given a deeper love, an invisible love. We recognize love based on our own values. Those who appreciate sweets will seek out or be given sweets. The sacred source easily gives us what we recognize according to our own karma.

But when our minds are purified and evolve—when we are softened by eternal love—we may experience love in all things, irrespective of their value. You are loved by the sacred source. To trust means to connect to the sacred source and receive love. We experience love from the sacred source and through our spiritual guides, who lead us on our evolutionary journeys.

# 96

## Magnetize goodness

A positive mental attitude attracts positive things. Negative thoughts unconsciously color our thinking and attract more negativity. As birds of a feather flock together, so our minds attract like a magnet what our minds focus on. To make use of this principle, it is important to evolve and awaken our consciousness, maintain a positive mental attitude, and make correct choices. Otherwise, we attract useless and sometimes terrible complications that make us suffer.

When we purify and transcend the ego through meditation, we naturally and effectively attract good things in life. When we evolve further, we are at peace and filled with love and gratitude. Purify your thoughts. You will only attract good things.

Samadhi allows us to cease the constant activity of the mind, transcend it, and become our True Selves. We are then at one with eternal existence and protected against negative energy at a lower level.

# 97

## Steadily do one thing

It is not difficult for many of us to work hard when we get immediate results or quickly benefit from them. However, it is not that easy to keep on doing one thing if we don't get those same quick results or benefits. When our willpower is weak, we easily get bored and distracted. But sticking to what we have started increases our willpower, concentration, and confidence, and helps us focus our energy. Samadhi meditation, for example, cleanses karma through the sacred sound of a mantra. We must continue to recite our mantra so that we foster the wave of the mantra within ourselves and merge with it. In due course, this opens the door to the manifestation of dreams and aspirations. We can only achieve this if we have faith in our mantra and the sacred essence that we find in a master. If our faith and trust are not solid, or if our willpower is compromised, we may give up in doubt.

The vibration of meditation creates transformative energy. Continuous meditation builds up this energy within the meditator. Unlike muscles that shrink when we stop working out, the internal transformation gained through meditation never diminishes.

# 98

## Transcend mind

We have to awaken our minds to become truly free from the prison of the mind. Going from a state of *having* to do something to *wanting* to do something is a step-by-step process.

Competitive thinking that compels us to want to be first or above others ultimately exhausts us. Successfully achieving something we desired and feeling good about it only satisfies the mind and the ego. If we remain at this self-gratifying level, we may someday lose interest in everything and experience depression. This form of competition is inevitable until we experience freedom.

If we want to evolve beyond self-defense and fear, we must transcend the mind. The heart lies beyond the mind and is filled with infinite love and power. If we go further, beyond the heart, we reach true freedom and are released from all attachments. We are finally able to simply be who we are.

## 99

### Joyous self exists deep within

Our True Self exists deep within each of us and is full of love, freedom, and joy. When the mind is stimulated by the senses, on the other hand, it manifests defensive thoughts and feelings like doubt, anger, and envy. This masks and obscures our True Selves. We are so accustomed to living through the senses and the mind that we have lost touch with our True Selves and believe that who we are is embodied in our mind and feelings. This keeps us from accessing our joyous self deep within.

Many of us also make judgments about what is good and bad simply through sensory impressions and assumptions. There is no profound wisdom here. It is an automatic reaction that we believe is necessary to survive. We can simply live as we are; however, we don't experience this since we assume that we are defined by the senses and mind. We believe that we are what we have accumulated through our various life experiences.

The truth is that we are all born as free, loving, genuine, pure beings. That is the state of our True Selves.

# 100

## Nothing external is eternal

We are often busy pursuing satisfaction and fulfillment by doing external things. Think simply of cleaning a house: we feel good after cleaning a kitchen and bedroom well. However, there may still be plenty of unfinished rooms in the home to clean that would require endless work. This applies to anything external, including our jobs or hobbies. When we are preoccupied with external matters, we are forever busy doing things. Along the way, we tend to forget about ourselves on a deeper level.

What matters is the development of a channel that fosters fulfillment from within. We all possess too much of everything. The mind is attached to material things, titles, social status, and small, cheerful experiences. It refuses to let them go. But nothing external is eternal. Everything vanishes sooner or later. Let us awaken our bodies and minds. Let us release things from within and clear away the inner clutter.

# 101

## Change misfortune into a great opportunity

In the last few years we have seen companies go bank-rupt and people laid off. Being visited by such sudden misfortune can be devastating and frightening. Howev-er, if you accept the loss of a job with appreciation, it can be a great opportunity. In fact, it allows us to start again and make our lives more creative.

This applies to any misfortune. For example, if something happens that cuts off our food supply, we might fear not having anything to eat for days. We might become panicked by the prospect of extreme hunger. This mindset is toxic and harmful. On the contrary, if we simply shift our minds and try to per-ceive the experience as an opportunity to rest and rejuvenate the body, we are filled with restorative en-ergy. Our mindset largely determines how things will unfold. Misfortune is a small price to pay for some-thing greater. It can be a cleansing process that frees us from attachments of the mind and transforms our way of thinking.

# 102

## Aim for the formless, not the form.

We often try to look perfect by acquiring things. We are busy keeping up appearances, and, in so doing, we sometimes repress distrust and anger to keep appearances and observe rules. We rigidly protect ourselves. However, the persistent repression of negative feelings can complicate our personality and make us disingenuous. It is exhausting to forcibly tame and manage the mind in order to talk and act nicely. Even if we manage to do so, repressed feelings can burst out at any time, undermining and potentially damaging our bodies, causing extreme illness.

Outer appearances don't matter. We must focus on the formless dimension beyond the mind, not the physical dimension. We human beings come from an infinite field where no form or thought exists. In order to return to this field, we need to release attachments and become our True Selves.

# 103

## Float in a womblike sea of love

When the mind compels us to fixate on the perceptions of others, we eventually become exhausted and dull, even if we might seem vibrant at work or social events. The clutch of the mind wearies us while the ego gets fulfilled. And since the ego is infinitely demanding, we are never rested.

If we experience heartfelt love at all times—even at work—and if we maintain a connection to our spirituality and to a higher level of consciousness with awareness at all times, we will not be at the mercy of the mind. Our True Selves lie beyond the attachments of the mind, where neither worry nor time exists. Our body and mind get purified and unified in this ultimate Now. It is extraordinarily relaxing and healing to be here in the present moment as if we were embraced by and floating in a sea of love, or weightless inside a womb.

# 104

## Human beings can enlighten

Animals have a natural ability to survive in the wilderness. Hawks can see far into the distance in their quest for food. Dolphins can hear ultrasonic waves as they swim in the sea. Cats can sense an earthquake and avoid danger with their superior agility.

Since we don't have this natural advantage in the wilderness, we have developed the mind to better survive. It is impossible for animals to become enlightened, but we can. Unlike animals, we can become spiritually awakened. Just as our bodies grow in size and develop in strength, we too can develop and transcend the mind. As we cleanse the body and mind and expand our awareness, so we can transcend them and return to our True Selves. We can encounter the truth. Himalayan wisdom lets us follow the same path as Buddha and Christ.

We must not consistently pursue ephemeral desires or easy conveniences. Instead, we should strive to be awakened to divinity and to a state of supreme consciousness. Our abilities bloom with this awareness and endow us with the capacity to live freely with love, power, and wisdom.

# 105

## Great treasures within

Everyone wants to shine and live happily ever after in great material wealth, but this form of fleeting fulfillment does not provide deep satisfaction. Very few women, for example, receive a marriage proposal from a "prince on a white horse." Nonetheless, if your energy is positive and sound, it naturally attracts people and events in kind.

Everything is a lesson. When something goes wrong, don't blame others. Instead, become more self-aware. This growth opportunity to encounter your True Self cultivates great depth and maturity. When you encounter your True Self, you radiate brilliance. You have great treasures within. Power, love, and wisdom spring forth when you accrue good karma and are aware of how you use and purify your mind.

# 106

## Body and mind is a truly remarkable gift

We take life for granted, but every single experience we have in life is a growth opportunity. We are living in the present: seeing, hearing, feeling, and tasting. We are alive within amazing sensory and mental dimensions. Let us be grateful for these gifts that originate from an infinite source.

Let us not complain and instead express gratitude for the body and mind that we have been given—a truly remarkable gift. Let us love the soul that exists deep within. This reverential and appreciative mindset cultivates respect and love for others. Living with love, gratitude, and greater awareness also produces clarity of mind. Commit trust, love, and gratitude to God, the divine essence that sustains all life. May you be filled with love.

# 107

## True positive

Many of us wonder what we really want to do in life. Modern society emphasizes self-identity and self-actualization. It focuses on strengthening and working the mind. This tendency creates pressure and suffering. If we force ourselves to be habitually positive all the time, we end up so worn-out that we even run the risk of depression and self-loathing.

It is important to be positive wherever we are. However, to blindly and habitually be positive on every occasion is merely a reaction of the mind. This is escapism and a form of self-defense: to simply view your mistakes positively and strengthen your ego without obliging yourself to look deep within and make truly necessary changes.

It is important to be creative and honest during the process of self-realization. This is the path to encountering the True Self.

# 108

## Who and what fundamentally are you?

Do you know who and what you really are? Where does your suffering and joy come from? What lies within? What is the origin of your body and mind? Your parents gave birth to you and gave you a name. You work and live in a community. You perform a duty and have a role. Take a moment and ask yourself: Is it the "true you?" When you are sick, do you really believe that the "true you" is sick? Is it not your body and mind that suffer, not the "true you?"

The body and mind are not the "true you." They exist on the surface. You may suffer, worry, savor, and rejoice, but, in fact, it is the body and the mind that experience all these feelings. The "true you" quietly observes the body and mind with detachment. The source of power behind the body and mind is truly you: genuine, pure, free, and serene. It is a part of God, the creator of all.

**The grace of Mother Nature:**
You are loved by the sky, the water, and the wind.

There are various levels of love, including possessive love, obsessive love, and unconditional love. The most familiar one is between a man and a woman. Men and women attract each other because God created positive energy and negative energy to create new life for the prosperity of humankind. However, when this energy combines with our desires, we pursue physical pleasures according to our karma and, thus, generate excessive attachments.

What many regard as love, including personal love, is often a limited type of love that demands reciprocation. It procures both joy and pain, and demands love, compliments, and recognition in return. Our egos use love in this fashion to fill the emptiness we might experience within.

We are generally reluctant to give things up for this reason and fear losing them forever. Theoretically, this may sound possible—yet love never goes away. We have infinite love within ourselves from inception, though we have lost our connection to it in our competitive society. We may be tempted to seek love from others for our own contentment and protection, but this is "give and take" obsessive love.

Let us release obsessive love and develop unconditional love through compassion and mutual understanding. We need to grow spiritually and transform our desires into true love. This is possible through meditation, purification, and the transformation of the mind. This is the path to releasing attachments and desires and becoming truly free.

When we purify and transcend the mind, we also open our hearts. We cultivate infinite, unconditional love. The more we transcend the mind, the more fully we become our True Selves and may share with others the unconditional universal love that comes from being one with the source.

# AFTERWORD

This book consists of 108 teachings. Some of them may touch your heart and some may not, but each contains a true message from the universe. Every time you open this book, it may touch your heart differently. I sincerely hope that you keep this book at hand and read it over as often as you can. This is particularly the case if you are in pain and need a comforting, healing message.

I also hope that you learn and practice sacred sound meditation. This is given to you in the form of a mantra at a Siddha diksha, a ceremony conducted by a Siddha master who cleanses you with blessings of higher energy. The sacred sound of a mantra protects and transforms you, bringing success and happiness.

There is love, wisdom, and power within us that is part of our divine essence given to us by the sacred source. However, access to these attributes is cut off when we disconnect from this source. It is further obscured by the overly zealous ego.

As a Siddha master who has reached the truth through ascetic training in the Himalayas, I am here to guide you on a journey of transformation to expand your consciousness and help you reconnect to the sacred source. This will ultimately open the door to encountering the truth, liberating yourself from suffering and creating a fulfilling life.

I sincerely hope you encounter the essence. I am here to help awaken you and guide you to the Light.

YOGMATA KEIKO AIKAWA
August 2012

# ABOUT THE AUTHOR

**Yogmata Keiko Aikawa** was born in 1945 in Yamanashi Prefecture, west of Tokyo. She developed an early interest in yoga and naturopathy, which led her to travels in Tibet, China and India. She was one of earliest promoters of yoga in Japan, and in 1972 she founded the Aikawa General Health Institute, where she taught her unique Yoga Dance and Pranadi Yoga.

In 1984, she met the Siddha Master Pilot Baba while he was in Japan to perform a public Samadhi. He invited her to study among the Siddha Masters in the high Himalayas. There she met Hari Baba, who guided her through the final stages of Samadhi.

In 1991, Yogmata performed her first of many public Samadhis, a supreme yogic practice in which one is sealed in an air-tight, underground pit without food or water for seventy-two to ninety-six hours. After her eighteenth public Samadhi, she received the title of Mahamandaleshwar, or Supreme Master of the Universe, from Juna Akhara, the largest spiritual training association in India. Yogmata is the first woman and non-Indian to achieve this status.

She and Pilot Baba have held public teachings and initiations throughout the world as part of the World Peace Campaign. She is currently working with the United Nations on a series of international conferences to further universal peace, sustainable living and the leadership of women. Yogmata's charitable work includes the Yogmata Foundation, which is dedicated to funding mobile hospitals to remote villages in India. Her global mission is to bring love and kindness to all.

Today Yogmata lives in Japan. She has published over forty books.

## Connect with Himalayan Wisdom

Email: usa@science.ne.jp
Twitter: @himalaya_siddha
Website: www.yogmata.com
Facebook: "yogmata"